I0212321

LESSONS
FROM
EVERYWHERE

LESSONS
FROM
EVERYWHERE

A Collection of Poetry
and Spoken Word

PJ

PHOENIX JAMES

LESSONS FROM EVERYWHERE

Copyright © 2022 Prince-James Harrison.

All rights reserved.

No part of this publication may be reproduced, distributed, or transmitted in any form or by any means, including photocopying, recording, or other electronic or mechanical methods, without the prior written permission of the publisher, except in the case of brief quotations embodied in critical reviews and certain other noncommercial uses permitted by copyright law.

For any questions about usage, please email contact@PhoenixJamesOfficial.com

First Edition: 2022

ISBN: 978-1-7396788-4-5 (Paperback)
ISBN: 978-1-7396788-5-2 (Ebook)

Cover Artwork & Design by Phoenix James.
Book Design & Formatting by Phoenix James.

Visit the author's website at www.PhoenixJamesOfficial.com or email him at phoenix@PhoenixJamesOfficial.com

DEDICATION

To all those everywhere
Who have learned
The lessons of life
On their journey
Those who are still learning them
And to all those yet to come
And experience them
To those here
Sharing their lessons
And to all those gone before
Leaving behind
Only what they've learned
And the ones who
Become the example and lesson itself
I hope this adds to your enlightenment

And to a young boy
A long time ago
From whom I have learned
My most important lessons
And of whom I'm still a student

Thank you for your openness
Your unresting willingness to learn
And for your invaluable teachings

I'm still hoping I haven't let you down
That you feel a sense of accomplishment
That this has made your time worthwhile.

CONTENTS

AN AUDIENCE FOR EVERY SHOW

It's all subjective
It's not necessarily good or bad
It's how ever who's receiving it
Feels about it
How it affects them
How it impacts them
Or not
And that's the beautiful thing about it
Because the universe works in a way
Where we're all energy
And there's people at different places
At different times
Feeding off
Whatever energy they're feeding off of
Sometimes they may hear the same thing
Ten times
But it's at that particular time
That tenth time
That they're in the right space
They're in the right energy space
To receive whatever that thing is
Whatever that message is
That vibe is
Whatever they hear or see

So I don't beat myself up
About what I share
If I'm happy with what I share
Or there's something I want to express
Or it comes to me
And I want to put it out there
I do that
Because I know that there's always
Going to be somebody
That's receiving something from it
Or if they don't today
They will tomorrow
You're shooting out into the universe
Without a target in a sense
But you're always going to hit something
There's always an audience for a show
That's something I like to remember
That every moment is something
And there's an audience for every show.

BETTING ON VENUS

Taking a nap on my sofa
I fell asleep into a dream
I was seated in-between people
In the front row
Of what would be considered court side
If it had been a basketball game
Except it was an empty large open floor
Across the other side of the floor
As far up as the low lighting
Would allow me to
I could see the stands
Filled up with people
The floor was empty
Except for a woman dressed elegantly
In a tight knitted knee length dress
Right in the centre of the floor
Dancing slowly
To the music that filled the hall
She danced as if she was the only one there
Just her and the music
She reminded me
Of the first person brave enough
To step onto the empty floor
At a crowded party

And just dance by themselves
The energy she created called to you
To your bravery
To your courage
To join her on the floor
To dance with her
While everyone watched on
All eyes on you
And her reaction to you
I was sitting
With a few people I seemed to know
I turned to a friend
Directly next to me
And said
She looks to me like she wants someone
To go and dance with her
I dare you to be the one
If she dances with you
I'll give you ten pounds
When you come back
To my surprise
He took on the challenge
And smoothly danced his way
Onto and across the floor towards her
All eyes watched on
As this dapper male figure

Moves into the centre of the floor
Into the spotlight
Where this mysterious woman danced away
With her eyes closed
As if in a private world of her own
The next thing I knew
They were both up close
In an embrace
Him behind her
And slow dancing away
To the music together
Like the last lovers on the dance floor
At the end of a party
Two girls that appeared to know each other
And know me
And seemingly a part of the small group
I was seated with
Were now sitting closer to me
Having moved
Into the area my friend had left vacant
By getting up to dance
We were all in awe
And fascinated at the spectacle
Taking place before our eyes
Feeling pleased with myself
I turned to the girls and said

Well, that was money well spent
They looked at me
And then looked at each other
And then looked back at me
As if in some sort of shock
And bemusement
At what they had just heard
What they'd deduced from what I'd said
Is that I had paid the woman on the floor
To dance with him
Before I could say another word
They were turning to others
And telling them just that
I began to get annoyed
And demanded
That they stop spreading rumours
That I paid her to dance with him
Because it wasn't true
And that's not what I meant
After the song ended
I remember the crowd
Applauding
And then it seemed
There was perhaps an interval
As lights came on
And people got up and shuffled around

6

The two slow dancing stars
Exchanged a few pleasantries
In the middle of the floor
And then he walked back over
To join our group
He appeared to be almost floating
As he walked towards us
He appeared somehow greater
Like a man
Who was just returning to earth
From a successful mission to Venus
I stood up smiling
And greeted him
With a proud and brotherly embrace
And placed the ten pounds in his hand.

COMING DOWN

Last night in a dream
I bumped into my mum
On the road somewhere
It was after some miscommunication
About which of us would collect a parcel
After talking about that briefly
We decided we'd walk together
To go and collect it
All I remember is us walking for a while
Talking as we went
It was no place I could say looked familiar
But I could say that at one point
It seemed like
The back of a school playground
That we were walking across
I then remember
Us being on top of a giant pile
Of what seemed like discarded junk
Bits of plastic and metal
And broken furniture
It was at least ten feet tall
I don't know why
We were standing on top of it
I just remember climbing down

And then helping my mum down
Back onto flat ground
Then I remember walking
Down a familiar street
Without my mum
Somewhere else
Attempting to make amends
With an old acquaintance
For the sake of peace
And goodwill and posterity
Next I find myself at the counter
Of a busy fast-food restaurant
I spot another figure from my past
Working away off to the side
In what appeared to be
Part of the kitchen area of the restaurant
He was another person I thought
It would be the perfect time
To make amends with
And bury the old hatchet
I walked over to where he was
And managed to get his attention
I don't know what kind of reception
I was expecting
But he came over to me
And greeted and received me

Just as friendly as a person could
It was as if all the years since
Had softened him
And I was speaking to someone new
It was as if I was standing on a bridge
I'd never tried to cross before
And the water flowing underneath
Had long washed all the bad away.

COMMUNICATIONS 450 YEARS AGO

I believe you just had to walk
And hope that the person was home
That they hadn't gone out
Onto a field somewhere
Doing something with their farmland
Which was like acres
And maybe you rode your horse
Or you walked on foot
Until you found them
It might have taken you four days
To find them
But it didn't matter
Because you knew nothing of smartphones
You knew nothing of computers
You knew nothing of telephones
You knew nothing of writing a letter
And posting it
That might have been on its way maybe
I don't know
But you would have just
Looked for that person
You have no way of contacting them
This is before the postal service
It's before computers

Telephones
Smartphones
What did you do
You just walked around for four days
Until you found them
How did it go down
When you had to find someone
But they could have been anywhere
They were without aeroplanes
So they didn't fly anywhere
So they weren't too far
There were no cars
So they didn't drive anywhere far
They would have been around
But what if they decided to travel
On foot for four days somewhere
And they weren't able to notify you
What would you do
I guess you just wouldn't see them
Or you just kept visiting
Visiting again until they returned
That's crazy
Imagine
What if they emigrated somewhere
Before transport

Before cars and planes and buses
People would just disappear
You'd have gone to where they live
Their little hut or wherever it was
And they would have been gone
From that vicinity
They would've taken their stuff with them
And suddenly be nowhere to be found
How did that work
That's quite fascinating
How did it work
When someone decided
They wanted to move somewhere else
How did they get around
I suppose they traveled less
I reckon they traveled shorter distances
Because they couldn't really cross the ocean
Well, then again, they did do that too
Because obviously they built boats
And made rafts and things
Sailing would have been another thing
That was pretty big then
It's amazing when you think about it
The distances
That they still managed to cover
I think there were more communities

Back then
I think people were more together
They couldn't rely on a mobile phone
To message somebody
So they had to keep people close
Messages had to be shared
And promises kept more
I imagine that they kept together more
They kept in their circles more
Because obviously if they did separate
They would have gotten lost
And no means of contacting each other
No cellphone
Can't get back home and email them
And say sorry I missed you
Even if they didn't have a phone
They would have had email nowadays
They would have had some kind of access
To the person through a computer
Or even to write a letter and post it
With the Queen's head stamped on it
Not even that existed
I guess it was just smoke signals
Or sending out the messenger birds
Carrier pigeons
I wonder how far back that goes

I'd love to take a trip back in time
Just to see
How communications worked
Just a comms exercise
Just to experience
How communications were
In the early hundreds
That'd be interesting
Let's say the sixteen hundreds
Or further back in history perhaps
I'm not too sure
Of all that was happening
In the sixteen hundreds
I couldn't really pinpoint
Where I'd need to land
If I went back in time
In a time machine
I'd probably do a bit of research
Before I went
To see what was going on
At that time in history
And then decide from there
Armed with that information
I think a lot of people of today
Would struggle with the sixteen hundreds
I think even the greatest historian

Would struggle with the facts
And real timeframes of things
I think even Google would struggle
Imagine
Anyone that's at Google now
Was not around
And anything that Google works on
Wasn't around
So where does all the information
Come from
Is it passed down
How far back can you really go
And have accurate facts.

DARK SIDE OF ONLINE DATING

I recently told someone
About the Match.com rapist
I don't know
If they knew about it or not
They didn't reply to the message
It's because they were talking
About dating apps
And saying that Tinder
Is not a dating app
And I was saying
Well it is
Because the point of it
Is connecting with people on there
And then meeting up for dates
She was saying
It was a hooking up app
It's not for dating
But they're all hooking up apps
If you think about it
It depends
On what the person on there
Is on there for
I was kind of explaining that
And she was saying

That Match.com
Is more of a dating site
If you want an online dating site
And I said
Did you hear about the Match.com rapist
He raped five women
And was jailed two years ago
I was explaining that
And trying to say
That it doesn't matter what dating site
None are necessarily better than the other
It's the people that are using them
They are just online platforms
And the people who are using them
Their intentions are their intentions
They can go on any of them they like
Maybe these types of men think
That they'll go on these other sites
That are supposed to be the better sites
Because they think
They may get better women
Or more gullible women
You might expect to find
an unsavoury guy
On Tinder
More than you would on Match.com

But then if that's the case
Then he might find himself
On Match.com
Because you as woman
You're going to be more unsuspecting
Because you think he may be decent
Because he's on there
Because only decent guys
Are on these "better" dating sites
Let's say
I wanted to sleep with a woman
On the first night
I'm going to be the same
On any dating site I go on
I'm not going to change
If I'm a serial rapist
I'm going to rape you
Via Match.com
Or Tinder
It's not going to make a difference
Maybe I'll have to pay a bit of money
To be on the paid dating websites
Which people believe
Sifts out the bad people
But if I want "quality"
I might pay a little extra

Just to be in the circle
Of those particular women
Those unsuspecting females
Who because I'm within
That "safe online dating space"
That "sanitary pool of safety"
For online daters
Won't view me as a potential predator.

EARLY NIGHTS

It's Saturday nights like this
The occurrence of a rare occasion
When I'm in bed before ten
Fed, watered and content
Nestled cosily between my sheets
Aware of the comforting stillness
Of my apartment
Emphasised by the coming and going
Of those to and fro
On the other side of my door
The sounds of a key
Unlocking the door
Of an apartment downstairs
Upstairs
A stairwell door closes behind someone
And the elevator pings
Signalling another persons arrival
The jingle of keys
The closing of doors
The ping of elevators
And the sound of footsteps
All seem to play on a consistent rotation
Outside my window
On the street nearby

The drone of the busy traffic can be heard
Frequently there's a siren
And a car horn
And the roar of a motorbike
They are distant
And nonintrusive
Fused with
The rotation of sounds within the building
They altogether add a warmth and pleasure
To my silent solitude
A cacophony of bliss
A symphony of peacefulness
Laying
Lazy
Listening
In the knowing
And pleased
That I don't have to play any part in it all
That I'm not required
To be an instrument in tonight's orchestra
That the band are playing on
Perfectly well
Without me.

FREEDOM OF LETTING GO

We hear the saying that no-one is perfect
People just say it
And it kind of loses its meaning a little bit
But when I realised
How true that statement is
That no-one is perfect
Like everyone's got their own shit going on
Everyone's got stuff that makes their lives
Less than perfect
It made me look at my own self
In a whole different way
And how I feel about myself
We downplay things
And we don't show our true selves
And we try to hide our situations
When I really realised the realness of that
It opened up so much for me
In terms of being able to share
Who I am
And let go of pieces of myself
And it just makes things so much easier
When you come to that realisation
That everyone's in their own shit
And everyone's got their own shit going on

And no-one has got it perfect
No matter what pretence they put up
That their life is perfect
And they've got no issues
And they put all the negative stuff
To the back
And present their best self
Or cover up
With some kind of pretty cover
To make it all look good on the outside
When I came to that realisation
And accepted that
And saw that for what it was
Which took a while
It made it so much easier
To reveal more of myself
And the stuff that was hidden away
That we hide away
It just made things so much easier
I know I'm a much better person for it
I live so much freer now
It's actually done a whole turn
And made me want to share even more
Because of how freeing it feels
To let go and share pieces of that
Bit by bit as you can

And letting go
And letting go
And letting go
And you want more of that freedom
It becomes almost like a drug
Feeling that feeling of exhaling
You can let go
Of another piece of something
That was weighing you down
That you were dragging for so long
Thinking that you have to
Put up this perfect exterior
This presentation
Everyone else
Is trying to show their perfect self
So you feel like
You've got to show your perfect self
Otherwise you're going to look
Or appear less than everybody else
It's a new world
It's a new world basically.

HAIR

I've had every hairstyle known to man
I've had orange hair
I've had fuchsia pink
I've had blonde
I was doing hairdressing at the time
Working in several hairdressers
And going to the afro hair and beauty show
Every year
And our salon was competing
In competitions
Hair was the thing
I didn't have to pay for it
So I was always getting my hair done
I had the Sisqó hair going on
At the time when it was hot
I had it all
I don't know if there's any hairstyles
I haven't had
The only thing I haven't had is weave
I haven't had a weave
I haven't had any finger waves
People that don't really know
Are surprised that guys have weaves
I think you'd be hard-pressed

To find a hairstyle a woman can have
That a guy hasn't had at some point
Or going to have
But I think they've pretty much
Done them all
Especially in America
And probably other parts of the world
That I'm not fully aware of
A lot of men commonly
Adorn feminine hairstyles
Or considered feminine
I don't think there's a hairstyle
That a woman has had
That some man hasn't had as well
I don't do anything with my hair anymore
I'm not so adventurous
And outgoing with my hair
It's just quick and easy
Shave it all
Good to go
Simple
Fits every occasion
That's just how it is now
And there's less hair now anyway
It doesn't grow as much
As it did at those times

I've got forty year old hair
As opposed to
Sixteen, seventeen, eighteen year old hair
There's less of it basically.

HARD-ON WHEN WE KISS

Something today I read
It said if a man
Doesn't have a hard-on
When a woman kisses him
That means he's not that into her
Well I'm a kissy guy
I like kissing
I'm into kissing a lot
So if I'm kissing you
And I'm into it
And we are kissing compatible
I will definitely have a hard-on
One hundred percent
And if I don't
Then I'm probably not that into you
But it's very rarely that I wouldn't
If I'm kissing you anyway
Or perhaps I'm kissing you
And the energy or the vibe
Is not connecting
That thing that happens
When you kiss someone
And it's not meeting
There's no meeting in the middle

There's no meeting of minds
In the kissing realm
I expect to have a hard-on
If I'm kissing somebody
And if I don't
I'm not that into you
I can definitely say
There's been times I've kissed somebody
And there wasn't that spark
That led to a hard-on
It's that spark that causes that hard-on
If that man is stimulated
Through that touch
That kiss
Those lips connecting
Whatever thoughts are in his mind
At that time
About that person
Not every man is just naturally
Going to have a hard-on
Just kissing a woman
Or kissing anybody
There has to be something else going on
That connects for him
For the blood flow and to start working
To start going to those parts

To form that hard-on
That's just how the body works
To my knowledge
I'm no bioscience expert
But I can tell you that much
If he's stimulated up there
He'll be stimulated down there
I've sat across the table with someone
Talking to them intimately
And without any touch
Had an instant hard-on
I can't think of a time
Where I've just had it
Just out of the blue
Just conversation
Nothing to do with anything intimate
Or sexy
Or anything like that
I can't think of a time like that
Where I've had a hard-on
But definitely when
The talk might be sexy
Romantic
Or we're exchanging a look
Or it's getting quite flirty
But there's no touch

We're just across the table from each other
There are times when I've had that
And that would basically be because
I'm into the person
They say men are visual
Men are like visual creatures
And I think we are
I think we are very visual
I've seen a few things
That have definitely got me going
I'll tell you what
When I'm into a woman
And I'm spending time with her
I don't even have to be touching her
To get a hard-on
It could be just thinking about things
Just getting those tingles
When I look at her
I could just stand back
Observe her
And just feel that tingly feeling
And then it starts
It starts going from there
The juices start flowing as they say
Men have juices too
Don't get it twisted.

HELPLESS DREAMS

There's two separate dreams
I had when I was sixteen
That I've never forgotten
Even until this day
In the first dream
I'm in a bathroom at the sink
Looking in the mirror
Brushing my teeth
Suddenly
One by one
My teeth start falling out into the sink
Whenever I think of it
I can remember
The fear and panic of that moment
That seemed and felt so real
And the sound of my teeth
As they each fell out of my mouth
And into the basin of the sink
In the second dream
I'm on the ground floor
Of the high rise tower block
I once lived in as a kid
There were two elevators
Facing each other

And a door that led to a stairway
All of which could take you up
To the twenty-first floor
Or anywhere in-between that
And the first floor
Through that stairway door
Underneath the stairwell
Sat an abandoned black baby
Wearing nothing but a nappy
And surrounded
By a few Tesco shopping bags
Filled with groceries
I don't remember now
If back then
I thought much into
What the meaning of it might be
But as I became a little older
I used to think
Maybe the baby
Represented one of my children
Now as a man
I've often thought
Perhaps the baby is me
In the fashion of getting old
And becoming a child again
Dependant

The metaphor for once a man
And twice a child
Whenever I think of it now
I think the baby in the dream
Could be me in the future
Abandoned
Left in the darkness
Helpless
And alone.

HUMANS ARE TO BLAME

In terms of human beings
I don't think it's any outside forces
Aside from human beings
It's all our fault
People like to think that sixty
Or seventy percent of us
Are raised with respect
And the other twenty or thirty percent
Are corrupt and make the rest of us cynical
Where we start to lose ourselves
Our moral compass
Our humanity
And our compassion
But what has happened
Where have we gone wrong
That has allowed that twenty percent
To be that way
That's going to be conditioning
They weren't born that way
We're still to blame
The parents are still human
And the parents of those parents
Are still human
So where did the conditioning come from

It's all within the human space
There's nothing outside of humans
That caused it
So I would say we're definitely to blame
For all of our ills amongst ourselves
How we treat each other
It's all the fault of our own
I don't think aliens came down
And made us how we are
I don't think it's any worse now
Than before
Actually I think
Social media has sped up a lot of things
And exposed a lot of things
And the lifestyle is now is faster
I think people want things faster
And they know they can get them
So they behave in certain ways
I think the internet
Has made a lot of things worse
I think you could blame that
But again
That's humans.

IF I EVER GET MARRIED

If I ever was fortunate enough
Blessed enough
To be considered for marriage
If I was considered worthy
By any woman
To be taken seriously
In that department
To be considered worthy enough
Of a union so special
I would want it to be something themed
I would want there to be
Something unique about it
I don't know if themed
Is the right word
But definitely something unique
Something not conventional
I don't know if it would be anything like
Some of the weddings you hear about
Where everyone is dressed up
As stormtroopers
And the bride its Princess Leia
And the groom is Han Solo
I don't know
If it would be anything as themed

In that regard
But I definitely
Would want it to be a unique wedding
Something that would be more
Than the conventional
Something that stands out
Not only for those that attended
But for both me and my wife
Something that we would remember.

IT PAYS TO BE GOOD

It always pays to be good to people
It always pays to be courteous
To be kind
To show love and respect
It always comes back around
There's something I did for someone
Over twenty years ago
And an opportunity
Has come up for me now
That person is able to offer me
Based on the fact
That I was just good to them
Twenty years ago
A small thing
But it has lasting effects
And it's amazing to see
To see that in action
How something you do for someone
Can matter twenty years later
How people don't forget
How you're able to benefit
From something you did long ago
Something I did for someone long ago
I'm in a position now where

Their assistance can help me a lot
Just because I was good to them
When they needed it
It's amazing really
They're in a position to help me
And had I not been good to them
It may have been quite different
Twenty years on
There's been a couple of occasions recently
I've seen that play out in my own life
And it's special
It's something to be noted
Note to self
Continue being good to people
Continue being kind
Continue being courteous
Continue being friendly
Continue offering help where you can
Continue continue continue
Sharing love
Sharing your light
Sharing your experiences
Sharing your energy
And insights
It pays to be good.

KARMA IS SO REAL

Do you think
Good things
Happen to bad people
And bad things
Happen to good people
What about Karma
Where does that play
In that whole thing
Karma kind of
Turns that on its head a little bit
If karma is a real thing
I very strongly believe in karma
I see it play out a lot
Unceasingly and without mercy
Even with myself
Other people
It really is a thing
Karma is not to be taken lightly
It could be ten years
It could be twenty years
Karma just is real
It will come back around
When you think you've got away with it
When you think you're home free

It'll be there waiting for you
At your door
Tap tap tap on the door
When you're just relaxing
With your feet up
Thinking
Yep, I got away with that
Tap tap tap
Karma is at the door
Telling you
You've got a debt to pay
Karma is so real.

KINKY NAUGHTY NASTY SEX LIFE

I was laughing with a friend today
That I must have done something wrong
In terms of getting the action
It's been a while
Since I've had that kind of
Kinky
Sexy
Naughty action
And I think
Even in any recent relationships
I can recall right now
It's not been that type of party
It's just interesting
I think to myself, wow
Because he was explaining to me
About someone he was with
And how it was
And what she used to do
Things that she does
Things that I remember
But that's like when I was younger
Like ten years ago
I'm thinking what have I been living
I know all this

44

Why am I not enjoying
These pleasures in life
What is going on with my sex life
Why am I not enjoying
These kinky pleasures
A woman who wants
To share herself with me
In all these filthy ways
The woman he was telling me about
I don't know anything else about her
Other than all the things she's done to him
In the shower
And all the things she's done to him
While he's sitting on the couch
And unzipping his trousers with her teeth
And her reach-arounds
When he's drinking some water at the sink
She's reaching around from behind
And doing things to him
I don't know anything about her day job
How intelligent she is
I don't know any of these other details
They're not important
In this kind of conversation
He just made me feel
Like I've been missing out

Like I've been living some sheltered life
I always make jokes about it
But he really made me feel like it's real
Like I'm being deprived
I've been in some cocoon it seems
I remember
All the things he's talking about
Man, the kind of sex I'm experiencing now
Wow
It's nothing like what he's been describing
I feel like I haven't done anything
I feel like I'm a virgin again
The woman he was speaking of
Is forty-nine
So he made me realise
That no
It's definitely not an age thing
It's nothing to do with age
I started thinking
Okay maybe the women I'm dating
It's an age thing
They're more or less around my age
So maybe it's a younger thing
It's women that are younger
That are behaving in these ways
That really appeal to me in bed

He really made me realise
No, it's nothing to do with age
It's to do with the women
It's to do with the type of woman
And what she's into
How free she is
And how much she's able to let go
And just be nasty.

LAST TIME I CRIED

Someone asked me
When was the last time I cried
I honestly couldn't remember
But I think it was when
I thought about my gran
That's the last time I remember crying
Because I think to myself often
That I wish I had the chance
Before she died
To say thank you
That was the last time I cried
Thinking that I will never be able
To say to her
Thank you for everything
Thank you
Now that I'm older and wiser
And appreciate things more
And people more
She's gone now
But I cried thinking
About the fact that
I won't ever get to say
Thank you
To her

For all the things
She did to me
For me
And taught me
That was the last time I cried.

ME TOO & THE UNTRUE

My view
On the whole "Me too" movement
I feel it's good
I'm not actually addressing the movement
I'm addressing what is happening
That has caused the movement
To come about
I feel it's good
That now people are being exposed
I feel it's good that we've reached a time
Where things
Can't be swept under the carpet
Like back in the day
Where obviously it was for so long
I think it's a good thing
That people can't hide anymore
Things are coming out
Which enables the "Me too" movement
To come about
People saying
Me too
It happened to me too
It happened to me too

People have a place
To come out and speak
And they have a platform now
Social media and the Internet
Has opened up so much
I think that has created the exposure
People can't hide anymore
The media
Is not in the control of a few people
Everyone's the media now
Everyone can put their news
And information out there
And be judged
And included in whatever thing it is
Or speak on behalf of someone
Or something
The light is there for everyone to use now
They can pinpoint or put a spotlight
On anything they want to
My other flip side to that is
That with "Me too"
You unfortunately also get
A lot of crying wolf mixed in with that
Where people have seen an opportunity
To jump on the bandwagon
For whatever reason

And tell untruths
Spread things that aren't true
Just to be included
Just to be in the light of that
The attention
And opportunity that brings
That's the not so good side about it
Unfortunately
That's my thought on it
As good as it is
It comes with its bad
It's good that these people
Are being exposed for their wrongdoing
But it's unfortunate
That people are also using it
To put people in positions
That they don't necessarily deserve to be in
Just because this thing is happening
And they've seen an opportunity to gain
From getting on their soapbox
And speaking out about something
That never even took place
Putting people and their lives
And careers in jeopardy
And in danger
Through falsehoods

I think that's the downside of it
And also because of that
I think it taints
What things like the "Me too" movement
Are supposed to be about
That and other movements like it or similar
Are supposed to be about women or men
Speaking out
About things that have happened to them
And some justice being brought
To those wrongdoings
To the people who have committed them
That it is being manipulated and misused
Is a tragedy for us all
Especially for those who are true victims
That's the not so good side unfortunately
In my opinion
I definitely feel
If it's proven that someone has lied
About something that happened to them
That they've been assaulted
Or that they've been approached
Or groped
Or whatever by a man
And they've been found out to be lying
I definitely feel

There should be some kind of penalty
Because if it's something
That's taken seriously
And this individual
This man
Whoever it is they're accusing
Is found guilty of this crime
He will be the one to serve time
To have some kind of punishment
By law
By whatever
So I feel it should go the other way
If the accuser is found out
To be lying about it
Saying that this person
Has done this to them
Or that to them
Then they should have to serve
Some kind of time
Or pay some kind of penalty
To the equivalent
Of what that man or individual
Would have been facing
Or perhaps not the equivalent
Just for lying
But definitely some kind of penalty

Because you're talking about
People's reputations
People's careers
People's livelihoods
Being affected
For something they didn't do
So if it's proven
That it was a lie
That it was all fabricated
There should definitely be some cost
There should definitely be
Some penalty to pay
Definitely
One hundred percent.

MERCY ME

Mercifully, I call it a wrap
Mercifully, I allow myself to call it a day
On what's been a positively productive time
During the hours I've been awake
I woke up this morning
With a mission in mind
To complete some work I had to do
But I fell down a rabbit hole
Researching something
And then researching another thing
Which then led to something else
All was not lost
All of my curious exploration
Resulted in the solving of a problem I'd had
Lingering on my mind
And had been trying to find a fix for
For quite some time
It's this breakthrough
That had made the day a triumph
And although I'd miserably fallen short
Of what I'd set out to achieve initially
It was sweetened by the glory
Of what I managed to accomplish
In its place

It's days like this that I want to keep going
To keep squeezing these miniature wins
Out of each hour
Down to the last minute
The small successes
Piling them up like little bricks
One stone on top of the other
Building them up like compound interest
I'm raising a tower
I take a moment to admire my progress
And it's days like this
That I don't want to go to sleep
That I want to keep going
Keep working
But my mental mind
Wants to do things further
Faster and greater
Than my physical body will allow
If I could make things
In the speed that my mind creates them
I'd be a walking miracle
I could take over not *the* world
But my world
If one by one
We could all conquer the little worlds
Turning and burning within us

The world would take care of itself
But with all that said
There is something to be said
For signing off for the day
Shutting up shop
Winding down and switching off
Turning off the light
When it's not quite midnight
But before that
Before you're completely exhausted
And can't muster enough energy
Or enthusiasm to get yourself up
And into bed
When it's a decisive and conscious choice
To draw a line under the day
And call it done
When you can underscore
An agreement with yourself
To walk away from working
Late into the night
By actually pulling away
As you pull back the covers on your bed
And get in and just lay there
In the quiet and stillness
While the world rages on outside
Listening

Calmly to your thoughts
While you're still wide awake
Enough to think
To picture
To process
To realise
That this mercy
Is another form of progress.

NEVER GOING BACK

Technology has taken over
It's like we value that more
Than we do sitting down
And having a conversation with a person
I went through a phase
I was so against technology
Technology is ruining our lives
The robots are going to kill us
And I still think they're going kill us
But now
I'm definitely more on the other side
Of how much it does for us
How beneficial it is to us
And how much we've gained from it
Some people are longing for the old days
They want the old days to come back
But they're not coming back
It's not going to go back
To rubbing sticks together
And smoke signals on the roof
It's not going back there
We have to kind of embrace
Where things are going
And get with it basically.

NEW WORLD

At Waterloo train station
Having breakfast
Whilst waiting for my train
Since it's been famously stated
To be the end of the world today
I figured
I better go with a full stomach
As there's no guarantees on food
Wherever we'll all end up
It's highly unlikely today
That we'll experience
Anything as dramatic as meteors
Falling out of the sky
Or the so called Planet X
Passing by earth
To kiss us and say Hi
And turn our world upside down
Or any major earthquakes
Or enormous volcanic eruptions
Or buildings
And bridges
Or whole cities collapsing
Or gigantic tsunamis
Or huge tidal waves
Several hundred feet high
Travelling at

Five hundred miles per hour today
Such things do happen
Of course
Some of which we've seen
In recent years
And others
In times long ago
But none will happen
Just because
Today
Has been specifically predicted
As the end of the world
We can relax
At least for now
We'll still get to enjoy
Our Christmas gifts
And food
And holidays this year
And New Years celebrations
And party plans
Don't have to be cancelled
Or put on hold
Until our next life
You probably won't even notice
Any change
At this current time at all
Unless you're
Let's say

Spiritually connected
And in tune with our universe
And used to paying attention
To the energies that surround you
On their many levels
On a daily basis
Therein lies where the changes
Regarding the ending
And new beginning will be
That is to say
There is a major transition
And planetary make-over taking place
It's more on a conscious
And spiritual level
That it will be noticed and perceived
Although
There are many that won't
Many will notice
Where doors before were closed
They will now be opened
Where voices were silent
They will now be heard
And there will become
An abundance
And fortitude and progress
Where there was none
Where there is now an end
There will be a new beginning

This newness
Relates to the beginning
Of the new cycle
Where one part ends
And another begins
This is what ancient cultures
Are referring to
In regards to the end of the world
It is also not exactly a new thing
It's been in the process
For a long time
It's time for taking place is now
Think of a pregnant woman
Who has been long going through
All the stages of pregnancy
And is now finally giving birth
Imagine her
As mother nature
And a new world being born.

NO SEX & STOLE ALL MY MONEY

When I was around eighteen years of age
I lived at the YMCA in Hornsey
For about a year
I was a resident there
And one night
Me and some of my friends
Went down to central London to a club
We met some girls there
And we were hanging out
And dancing
Having a good time
And one of them
Ended up coming back with me
To my room at the YMCA
Imagine I'm 18 at this time
I've only been exposed to
Certain amounts of life
Not all of it
You know
We think we know everything at that age
This girl
Had stayed over the night with me
Didn't give me any sex
That's what I was hoping for

That was the whole plan
I was thinking
Yeah this girl is going to come back
I'm going to get laid basically
That was the idea
That didn't happen
We just ended up sleeping
I had a wallet on the shelf
You know where this is going right
I had a wallet on the shelf in my room
Where we were
Not far from the bed
She wakes me up in the morning
And says I have to go now
We say our say goodbyes
I'm still half asleep
It was a heavy night
I was tired basically
So she's heading out
I remember I didn't get anything
So there's that
I say goodbye
And I think
She kissed me on my forehead
Or something
As I was half asleep

66

I don't remember exactly
Then she left
I woke up some time later
And when I'd eventually got up
Fully woken up and everything
And looked around
And I looked in the wallet
I found that the last
Forty pounds
I had to my name
Was missing
It was the last forty pounds I had
To last me quite a while
She had taken that forty pounds
And disappeared
Into
I won't say the night
Because it was the next day
Disappeared
Into the outside world basically
Gone
Vanished
Never ever to be seen again
I don't think I could tell you
What this girl's name was
It was just one of those little things

That came to mind
About not knowing who you're dealing with
And who you're inviting into your space
And into your life in general
That was a lesson that now looking back
I'm glad I had and I can recall as a lesson
At the time I wasn't as happy about it
Obviously
But it really taught me a lot about people
And how people can be
And the whole thing of being deceitful
And cunning
And conniving
At eighteen
A young impressionable teenager
That was a lesson to learn
Realising that not everybody
Is a good hearted person
Well-meaning
That definitely affected my trust level
In terms of bringing women or females
Back to my humble abode
That was a necessary lesson
I could have reported it
I didn't
I just took it

I accepted it
When you're young
You just think
You're probably not going to bother
So I took it as a loss
I was mad
But there was going to be no finding her
She didn't leave any trace
So that was that really
I don't even know if it happened now
Which it's not likely to
If I would bother reporting it
I mean it's a classic case of
Well, you brought a stranger
Back to your place
What do you expect
So that was a lesson there I learned early
Not to be so trusting around strangers
It could have been worse
You don't know who you're dealing with
I'm lucky it was forty pounds
It could've been my life she took
So yeah, man
Got to be careful out there.

NOTHING BEFORE IT'S READY

My day has been good
I'm just here thinking
You can't help everybody
You know that saying
You can lead a horse to water
But you can't make it drink
It's so true
There's only so much advice
You can give someone
It's not about the person
Not being capable
Of being completely stupid
It's just about
The just not being in that space
To receive
What you're giving them yet
I like to look at it as seeds
It's a seed that will later grow
When the soil is ready
The seed isn't going anywhere
Because it has been planted
When the soil is ready
Then it will grow
Then it will sink in

And grow
Into something beautiful hopefully
I just felt a little bit drained
From giving that energy
And it just falling on infertile ground
Infertile soil
It's just the way it goes sometimes
I can't help but give
But sometimes
The soil is not ready basically
So I'm just refilling
So I can give more
It's been a good day
I've been reminded
How important it is to give and refill
And that the soil is not always ready
You're pouring the water out
Putting in the seed
But the soil isn't ready
And nothing
Is going to make that grow
No sunlight
No soil
Not water
Nothing is going to make that grow
Until it's ready to grow

Until something is ready to grow
Nothing is going to happen
That is today's lesson.

OLD PHONES WERE BETTER

I still prefer the old way
Of hanging up the phone
These new phones don't let you do it
It's not the same
You don't get the same feeling from it
Or produce the same effect
A good old fashioned rotary phone
With a handheld receiver
You could really let someone know
How you felt
Just in the way you hung up the phone
They were sturdy too
Like they were made
With hanging up in mind
I miss that
You have to do too much explaining now
Too much unnecessary typing
Hanging up the old fashioned way
Said everything you needed to say
It punctuated exactly how you felt
And the end of the conversation perfectly

*Yeah, well you can shove it, I don't need
your stupid job anyway* - SLAM!

*We agreed 5 o'clock, what makes you think
I'd still be standing there waiting for you
at six, fool* - SLAM!

*Yeah, well good, I was never really into
you anyway* - SLAM!

*I'm telling you now, I'm done talking,
when I come there, you better have my
money* - SLAM!

I don't like these new phones.

OVERSEXED

You see
The problem we have today
Is that our children
Our teenagers
Our young people
Are over sexualised
By the media
Before they even
Know how to add up
Numbers properly
Or how to write
Or even speak
Or communicate properly
They're flooded with images
It's all in what they see
And hear
These articles of sex
These images of sex
Or sex related
Sex driven media
It's on their televisions
At home
It's in the movies they go to see
In the music they listen to

The magazines
They pick up and read
They get home
They jump onto the internet
And it is saturated with all of that too
Their friends
Are talking about sex
And with technology today
A child
Can carry all of this stuff
Around with them
In their pocket
Or their purse
Everywhere they go
Everyday
All you need
Is a smart phone
And you have instant sex appeal
I'm telling you
People will know what I'm talking about
What I'm saying is
You have to expect
When you talk to a child
On the street today
About church
About god

About religion
About spirituality
About fornication
About the sanctity of marriage
Or anything
In the realms of righteousness
Or godliness
You have to take these things into account
Because guaranteed
The majority of young adults today
Will be either
On their way to
Or coming from
An activity
A meeting
A conversation or something
Centered around
Or stemming from
The subject of sex
Or sexual relationships.

This is a dialogue segment from the Phoenix James written, produced and directed, feature length mock documentary film, Love Freely but Pay for Sex, released in 2013.

PASSING THROUGH

There's so much more meaning to life
Than to spend it in quarrelling
Than to spend it in strife
Disagreeing with him, her, and you
There's too little time
And far many better things to do
When we're all only passing through

There is so much beauty too brief
And abundant wonders too short
More worthwhile to view
The minutes in a day are too few
To spend in trouble, and discord with you
When we're all just passing through

Our collected rage and passions all subside
This is the making and nature of time
As fate calls in on you and I
To leave them each and all behind
All things too decay and die away as they do
And we, are all just passing through.

PHARMACY

Last night I dreamt I was in supermarket
Late night shopping with my mum
We were at the checkout counter
I was speaking to a woman on the phone
Yesterday afternoon before the dream
I had walked down the high street
From my apartment to my local pharmacy
The sun was shining
And the weather was the warmest
It had been so far for the year
I approached a man
Who was stocking a bottom shelf
And asked where the Lactulose was
He told me it's kept behind the counter
And that I could get it from someone there
As he pointed over to a large counter
At the back of the store
I joined a queue
And stood waiting third place in line
A fidgety small boy
At the front with his mother
Turned and breathed into her face
And said
See?!

Seemingly impressed with himself
Her reaction however
Was one of annoyance
As she shrugged him off
A second woman
One place in front of me
Stood holding a pram
With a small baby sleeping inside
And looking at her phone
With her stood a young girl
Taking off her jacket
And stuffing it into her rucksack
After a while
A woman behind the counter
Called me over to be served
I asked her for Lactulose
As she took it from the shelf
And placed it on the counter
I asked her
If there was anything else similar
Or like it that she could recommend
She turned back to the shelf
And suggested Senokot
Alternatively to that
She also suggested a box of suppositories
I decided on a box of suppositories

Which she placed on the counter
With the Lactulose
I said I'll take both of those
She said she'd have to check whether
They could both be bought together
She checked
And told me it says I can
With a slight smirk
She advised I didn't take both together
I joked and replied
What if you needed quicker results
She said something about other people
Needing to use the bathroom
I responded
But what if you live on your own
Then it's okay
She laughed and said
Just make sure you have a gas mask
She then recalled a time
She had to use a laxative
And her son then being worried
About the smell
And afterwards
What state the bathroom would be in
I don't remember how
We got onto taking about airplane toilets

But we both agreed
On a plane flight is probably
One of the last places
You'd want to succumb
To the effects of a laxative
With no guarantees
You could get access to the toilet
When you needed it
I finished paying for my items
As we exchanged the last
Of our pleasantries
And I exited the pharmacy
Back onto the warm sunny high street
She is the same woman I was speaking to
On the phone in my dream last night
Standing at the supermarket checkout
With my mum
I was asking her
If there were any jobs available
At the pharmacy
As we spoke I also remember her saying
That she was now at her second job
I don't recall now
What she said she did
At that second job
But I do remember asking her

If there were any jobs there too.

PROPOSITIONED

Her first proposition for the day
I feel women get propositioned every day
I think about myself
I can say once a week at least
Or twice a week
As a good-looking guy
Nothing really wrong with me to look at
They don't know I'm crazy
They have no idea
They're just looking from the outside
So I get propositioned
At least once a week
I can say I get that
I couldn't imagine
What it's like for women
I imagine women
Get propositioned every day
Every few blocks
Every place they enter
In every place they go
At work
Meeting friends
Hanging out
I imagine

They're getting propositioned
Very often
I say the average woman
Is getting some kind of proposition
From some guy
Or woman
Quite often
At least once a day
I imagine women
Are being propositioned
By somebody
I'd like to know if that's true.

REQUIREMENTS FOR PERMANENCE

The day that I would tattoo
A woman's name on me
We would have to have few kids together
We would have to be committed
In a long-term relationship
If not married
Living together and all the things
That go along with that
Someone that's going to be
A part of my life forever
Marriage
Living together
We have children together
Everything
We're going to be basically
A part of each other's lives forever
It would have to be something really deep
Long-term
Children are involved
Marriage is involved
Some long term commitment is involved
For me to consider that as a realistic thing
That I would do
To tattoo a woman's name on my body

I would have to be head-over-heels
Really head-over-heels
I don't even know how to describe
How I would have to be
For me to actually go
And tattoo a woman's name on me
She'd have to be
The last thing I think of going to bed
She'd have to be
The first thing I think of when I wake up
Just my everything
She would have to be out of this world
Forsake all others
Until death do us part
I worship the ground she walks on
She would have to be something special
For me to even consider it
Unfortunately I haven't met anyone
That I feel that way about yet
To want to have their name
Permanently tattooed in my skin
Forever and ever
It would have to be super special
More than super special
It's just a lot.

SAVING THE DAY

How it is with me
I need something
Even if it's just one small thing
To make my day feel productive
If it hasn't been already
Generally it is
But if it hasn't been as productive
As I would like
It's like I need something
That can save the day
One small thing that I can bring to my day
Or something that happens
That I wasn't even expecting
That makes my day feel like
Ah that's better
I was feeling like
I didn't get the most out of the day
That I could've got
Or it was feeling like
It was coming to an end
And I didn't achieve anything in my day
I didn't feel productive enough
There has to be some little something
A little piece of something

That either takes place
Or that I create
That makes my day feel worthwhile
If it's not my usual day
If it feels like it's coming to the end
And I haven't achieved much
There needs to be something to happen
Or that I make happen
That saves the day
Otherwise I feel down
I feel like I didn't get the most
Out of this day
I feel like I need to
So that's why all my days are like that
All my days are focused on productivity
Because I feel my best
When I'm producing
And things are happening
I feel like that was a great day
Another productive day
Yes
Another one in the can
But when it's feeling like
It's not as productive as it could be
And it's coming to the end of it
And I'm not seeing any sign

Of how
I'm going to make productivity happen
It's not a nice place
So what I do then
Is make the motion
To make something happen
It could be very simple
It could be a phone call
It could be writing something
That I needed to do
Or whatever
Just some motion that saves the day
Or a vlog
Or something
Something to correct that feeling
Or save me from despair.

SECRET SPY

My third floor apartment
Is one of only four of its kind
Within my entire block
These four apartments are unique
Because they have two levels
Upstairs and downstairs
All of the other apartments
Have only one level
One door in, same door out
Both levels of mine
Have a door each that I can enter
And exit my apartment from
So technically I live on two floors
Third and fourth
Which also means
I have two sets of neighbours
My upstairs neighbours
And my downstairs neighbours
My upstairs door
Is more like a back door
It's not any different
From my downstairs door
Except I barely use it
My downstairs door

Is what I call my front door
It's where I enter in
And out from most frequently
Both doors though are identical
And work in exactly the same way
Separate keys for both
Both with spy holes to see out of
The only difference
Is one unlocks and opens
From the left side of the door frame
And one unlocks and opens
From the right side
I often think
I should exit and enter the elevator
From the fourth floor occasionally
Just to change things up
To use my upstairs door more
Also to have a greater idea
Of who my upstairs neighbours are
Like I do with my downstairs neighbours
As I tend to see them coming and going
More often
Sometimes if I'm not occupied
I'll look through my spy holes
Both upstairs and downstairs
When there's activity outside either door

And see who's coming and going
So I'm already familiar with a few voices
And faces
And their visitors
And their habits and lifestyles somewhat
It's funny to think
My upstairs neighbours
Come and go everyday
Past my upstairs door
And have no idea who lives there
As they've never seen me
That I know snippets
And soundbites of their lives
And they know nothing of mine
When I'm upstairs
I mostly feel like a secret agent
Like some kind of secret spy.

SEX AT THE NATIONAL GALLERY

I once had sex in the National Gallery
In the disabled toilets
It was fabulous
But after we'd finished
A lady was trying to get in
They were also baby changing toilets
She was trying to get in
To change her baby
So what happened
From outside
She'd managed to unlock the door
And there we were
Both still laying on the floor
Just finished enjoying ourselves
Her still straddled on top of me
Both only partially clothed
And the lady just stood there
In front of her baby's pram
With the door open
And the look of shock on her face
She closed the door again
We got up off of the floor
Pulled ourselves together
And got fully dressed

After that we exited the toilet
I half expected to see the woman
Still waiting outside the toilet
But she had seemingly disappeared
Nowhere to be seen
I remember on our way out
We walked past a security guard
I can still see her face now
Standing at the door with her pram
And seeing me and this girl
Laying on the floor
She was on top of me
Cowgirl position
What was funny
Is that from the door
The woman could only see my face
She couldn't see the girl's face
Because the girl was facing me
With her back towards the door
So she couldn't see the woman either
When the woman opens the door
Our eyes make four
At that moment
It's just me and her
There I am
Caught

On the floor of the toilet
Of the National Gallery
Trousers around my ankles
And her staring over me
All this woman wanted to do
Was to use the toilet
And see to her baby
That was many years ago now
I still think it's hilarious.

SEX ON A PLANE

Someone asked me what's my fantasy
I'd love to join the mile-high club
That would be one of my fantasies
It would be the adrenaline of it
And thinking that you're doing it
In the sky
That's sexy
I think there's something to that
Why wouldn't you want to do that
Why would you just want to do it
On the earth
On the flat earth
Who wouldn't want to do it in the mid air
That's just nuts if you don't want to
If you've had the opportunity
And you haven't
Then I think you've missed an opportunity
I think it's one of those things
That should be on everyone's bucket list
I want to join the mile-high club
I'd like to feel if there's any difference
In the feeling of gravity
If there's any added sensation
To being in the air so high

I'd only get to find out by doing it
That's my excuse
I just want to explore gravity
Sex on a plane
It doesn't have to be a plane though
It could be a rocket
I'm not ruling out riding on a rocket
Literally.

SOGGY CORNFLAKES

I went to school in Barbados
I used to live with my gran
And my great-gran
When I was getting ready for school
My gran would make cornflakes for me
With hot milk
And I don't know what happened
I don't know if I ever liked it
Or if there became a period
Where I didn't like it anymore
But what I used to do
I had this plastic bag full of my toys
That was underneath the dining table
I used to pour the soggy cornflakes
Into the bag
And it accumulated over time
Until it was all green and mouldy
Inside this bag
I don't think I was even ten yet
I used to pour this soggy cornflakes
Into this bag under the table
Pretending that I had eaten it
One morning
My great-gran

Was taking out the rubbish
She asked me if there any more rubbish
I saw it as an opportunity
To get rid of the bag
So I gave my great-gran the bag to take out
The bag of evidence
Full of my mouldy toys
To throw out with the trash
And then I would never get caught
I'd have got rid of the evidence
I don't what happened after that
As far as I remember
The bag was no more
And that was the end of it
My gran and great-gran
Have since passed on now
It was only recently
That my mother told me a story
That my gran had told her back then
About how I used to take the bowl
Of cornflakes and warm milk
And pour it into a bag
Stored underneath the dining table
It turns out in this case
I wasn't the only one
That knew my secret.

STRANGE DREAMS

Last night I had a strange dream
I was involved in a kind of TV game show
Lots of gay celebrities
Sitting in rows of seats
Everybody was dressed up
Made up in make-up
In a buzzing and busy TV studio
Cameras and bright lights
I don't know what any of it means
The night before
I had another strange dream
I was the leader
Of a very large group of people
They looked to me for guidance
As I navigated the crowd through streets
And across busy roads of traffic
At one point
In my arms, I was carrying a baby
I don't know who it belonged to
Before that I was shielding my mum
From being crushed
By the surge of the crowd
We were all making a pilgrimage
From one place to another

I don't know from where to where
We seemed like travelling refugees
I've been having these strange dreams
And I don't know what they mean.

THE SEX BETTER BE DAMN GOOD

He expected to plan it out
Over a period of time
How he was going get the sex
But he got there
With his plan
And she
Would already have her own plan
Of getting it a lot sooner
Than he had anticipated getting it
She pretty much had her legs open
And he was not prepared
If a man is planning his strategy
Of how he is going to get into
A woman's underwear
And he is put off
Because she was too fast
Man, she must be fast
She'd have to be pretty fast
For him to be put off
By her offering it to him on a plate
She's Speedy Gonzales in that department
We know men want it
Men like it
I like it

So if a woman is offering it to me
It makes it easier
But for me to be put off
She's offering that way too fast
Something's wrong with it
I don't want it
If it is just sex
Keep them interested
If that's all that he's there for
The best hope
Is to give it to him really good
Really really good
If he's only there for sex
And you're hoping to keep him
You better be good
What you give him better be really good
Because he ain't coming back
If it ain't good
It's no guarantee
That he's going to come back anyway
But if you're trying to keep him
Give it to him damn good
Because then
You've got more of a chance
Of keeping his interest
If that's all he's there for

It better be good
Like a meal
It better be finger-licking
If that's all he's there for
And it's not good
He ain't coming back
You're not going to keep him
If you know that's all he wants
But you still want him to come back
Then that one thing he's interested in
Better be really cream of the crop
You better make sure
That you're on your a-plus game
That's the only way it's going to happen
You've got to be on form
With excellence
He better not
Have experienced
Anything like that
In his life.

THE TIME I TRIED JAMAICAN WEED

Once I tried some weed in Barbados
I tried some Jamaican weed
And do you know
I slept for half the day at the beach
I slept so strong
That I woke up
And my shoes were gone
My shoes were gone
And my socks were gone
And I had to walk home bare feet
Some strong Jamaican weed, man
I can't even tell you
I don't even know when it happened
And when it took place
I just know
That I was out for the count
When I woke up
I don't even know where I was
I swear to god, man
I had to walk home bare feet
Like seriously
And I will never forget that
That Jamaican weed is strong, man
It's no joke

Worse when you're not a smoker
And you're trying it like me
I'm not a weed smoker
But I definitely remember
Smoking that weed
I don't think it agreed with me at all
I don't know
If because I don't smoke weed
If I was more of a lightweight
And it affected me in a bigger way
Than it would a normal weed smoker
But I'll tell you what
I don't forget it, man
I don't forget that day.

THEORY OF DESTINY

I think it's a wonderful design
I know we can plan
And do things
And direct things
But I think there's a greater plan
And it's only different
In regards to whichever route
You choose to get there
I think destiny is already planned out
It's all mapped out already
The choices we get
And which route we're going to take
To get there
But we're going to get to that end thing
That's already mapped out already
It's like we get to a fork in the road
And we have to make choices
Of which route we're going to take
But ultimately
It leads to the same place in the end
I think so
I'm still playing with it in my head
I don't know
And then I have a feeling

I deeply believe we have the power
To change every aspect of our lives
Maybe we are empowered to change things
But still where it leads to is the same place
We just choose which route we take
It feels like it's a different route
Than the other one we would have taken
Which it is
But ultimately
We end up with this place
That's planned out for us
Like who we're meant to be with
And where we're meant to live
I'm not firmly fixed on that
It's just a theory
An idea that I play with.

THINGS I WISH I DIDN'T HAVE TO DO

I'm looking forward to my bed
I am looking forward to sleeping
I'm looking forward to my bed
Like I'm going to Disneyland or something
I'm so excited
About jumping into the sheets
I feel my favourite part today
Is going to bed
I am looking forward
To diving in there
Like it's a swimming pool
Off the diving board
That's how I am going to land in my bed
Usually
It's something I don't look forward to
Having to go to sleep
You want to keep going
But you know you should sleep
You know you have to get rest
You know it's important
But you kind of hate it
Because you know the hours
That you are not going
To be being productive

Those awake hours
Sleeping will be productive for
Your immune system
And your resting
But it won't be productive
For getting stuff done
Like work-wise
So I hate those things
I hate that we have to do them
Like going to the toilet
I hate that I have to go to the toilet
I hate that I have to eat
I hate that all that time
Is happening to be used up
For those things
It's too much time going to the toilet
Too much time sleeping and eating
When you add it all together
Over the period of a year
Do you know how much
I could have got done in that time
I'm just vexed
When I have to stop what I am doing
To go and eat
Because I know time is being taken away
From what I was doing

If I could do away with them
And didn't have to do any of them
I'd be so happy
There was this thing I heard
Or read or saw somewhere
About how much time we spend
During our twenty-four hour day
Eating
Sleeping
Going to the toilet
And the basic human things
That you have to do in a day
It said the amount of time
We actually spend outside of that
Like actually living
And enjoying life
Was so small in comparison
To all the years that we spend
Doing those other things
Work
Sleep
Eating
And so forth
It said that the time
Was so minuscule when compared
It was kind of scary

To think that half of our lives
We're alive
But not really living
Just doing things we have to do
It was kind of saddening a little bit
To think that we spend so much time
Doing these other things
That we just have to do
It's not because we want to do them
Think of all the time we've wasted sleeping
Throughout our lives
We've wasted away our whole lives sleeping
Or eating
Or sitting on the toilet
On top of all the other things
That we procrastinate with
And waste time with
And get distracted by
And we think to ourselves

Oh man
I wasted so much time on that
I've could've been doing better things

I wasted so much time
With that person

Why did I watch that stupid program
That show is such trash TV
Car crash TV

I'll never get that hour back.

WORLD IS FINE

The
world
is
fine

Humans
are
the
problem.

ABOUT THE AUTHOR

Phoenix James is an award winning Writer, Poet, Author and Spoken Word Recording Artist. He began performing his poetic words live on stages across the UK in 1998. His debut spoken word poetry album, *The A.R.T.I.S.T,* was released in 2000. His first limited edition printed collection of poetry, *To Whom It May Concern,* was published in 2003. He has toured and performed his poetry internationally since 2004. He has appeared in films, on television and radio shows, and collaborated with other artists, singer-songwriters, actors, musicians, filmmakers and producers. In 2013, he wrote, directed and produced the feature length mock documentary film, *Love Freely but Pay for Sex.* Phoenix James has written, recorded and released several spoken word poetry albums including, *Phenzwaan Now & Forever* (2009), *A Patchwork Remedy for A Broken Melody* (2020), *FREE* (2021), *Haven for the Tormented* (2021), *With All That Said* (2022), and *Remixes* Volumes: 1 & 2 (2022).

If you enjoyed reading this book, please leave a review online. The author reads every review and they help new readers discover his work.

PHOENIX JAMES

Photo by Phoenix James

Phoenix James lives in London, England.

Connect with Phoenix James on his online social media platforms via www.linktr.ee/Phoenix_James and say you've read this book. To contact or learn more about Phoenix James and his creative journey or to receive updates via his Newsletter Mailing List, visit his official website at www.PhoenixJamesOfficial.com

CHECK OUT THE AUTHOR'S OTHER
BOOK TITLES ALSO AVAILABLE
IN PAPERBACK & EBOOK

PHOENIX JAMES
POETRY & SPOKEN WORD
COLLECTIONS:

**LOVE, SEX, ROMANCE
& OTHER BAD THINGS**

ROUTE TO DESTRUCTION

DELIRIUM OF THE WISE

**DON'T LET THE
DAFFODILS FOOL YOU**

CALL ME WHEN YOU'RE FREE

FAR FROM THE OUTSIDE

THE ONES WE DIDN'T KILL

DISCOVER THESE AND MUCH MORE
AT PHOENIXJAMESOFFICIAL.COM

Phoenix James Official

www.ingramcontent.com/pod-product-compliance
Lightning Source LLC
Chambersburg PA
CBHW021238090426
42740CB00006B/596